Joh

By United Library

https://campsite.bio/unitedlibrary

Table of Contents

Disclaimer

This biography book is a work of nonfiction based on the public life of a famous person. The author has used publicly available information to create this work. While the author has thoroughly researched the subject and attempted to depict it accurately, it is not meant to be an exhaustive study of the subject. The views expressed in this book are those of the author alone and do not necessarily reflect those of any organization associated with the subject. This book should not be taken as an endorsement, legal advice, or any other form of professional advice. This book was written for entertainment purposes only.

Introduction

Step into the intellectual world of John Locke, the brilliant English philosopher and physician whose ideas ignited the Enlightenment era and forever transformed the landscape of modern thought. In John Locke's book readers will embark on a captivating exploration of Locke's life, philosophy, and far-reaching influence.

Born in the 17th century, Locke's ideas laid the foundation for the Enlightenment's emphasis on reason, individual rights, and the pursuit of knowledge. This comprehensive biography delves into Locke's remarkable journey, from his early years as a student at Oxford to his later role as a prominent thinker in the court of William III.

Locke's groundbreaking contributions spanned multiple domains, making him one of history's most influential figures. His theory of the mind as a "blank slate" revolutionized our understanding of human cognition, paving the way for later philosophers like Rousseau, Hume, and Kant. His concepts of empiricism and the rejection of innate ideas challenged prevailing notions of knowledge acquisition.

Delve into Locke's profound impact on political philosophy, including his foundational work on social contract theory. His ideas on limited representative government, the protection of rights, and the rule of law continue to shape modern democracies and are echoed in foundational documents like the United States Declaration of Independence.

This book offers readers a rich tapestry of Locke's life and ideas, drawing connections to his contemporaries and tracing the legacy he left for subsequent generations. Whether you are a seasoned scholar or a curious reader, this book invites you to explore the enduring contributions of a philosopher whose principles continue to resonate in the realms of philosophy, politics, and human understanding.

John Locke

John Locke, born August 29, 1632 in Wrington (Somerset) and died October 28, 1704 in High Laver (Essex), was an English philosopher. He lived during a pivotal period that saw the end of the Wars of Religion, the beginnings of rationalism and strong opposition to absolutism in England. A close friend of the Earl of Shaftesbury, Locke took part in these debates and in the then nascent theories of the social contract, law and natural law, and the state of nature. He was also interested in the beginnings of what would come to be known as liberalism from the 19th^e century onwards.

His writings on tolerance cannot be dissociated from a period in which a profound readjustment of the political and religious fields was taking place. In the viewpoint partly opened up thanks to him, politics was concerned with the present world and religion with the world beyond, and the two should not interfere. His political theory was opposed to the absolutism then being established in France, which failed to take hold in England, partly because of him. He was also one of the founders of the notion of the rule of law.

His *Essay on Human Understanding* is a major work in which he constructs a theory of ideas and a philosophy of mind. While opposing Hobbes' materialism, he considered experience to be the origin of knowledge, and rejected Descartes' notion of innate ideas. His theory of knowledge is called empiricist.

Alongside his philosophical activities, he was one of the main investors in the Royal African Company, a pillar in the development of the slave trade.

Biography

Training years

John Locke was born near Bristol on Sunday, August 29, 1632. His father, a solicitor, owned houses and land in Pensford, near Bristol. During the Civil War, he served as a cavalry captain in the service of a parliamentary army. His regiment was commanded by an influential Somerset man, Alexander Popham. Although this army was defeated and dispersed in July 1643, Locke Sr. remained close to his regimental commander, Alexander Popham, who became MP for Bath in 1645. It was thanks to Popham that John Locke was able to enter the highly reputed Westminster School in 1647. There, Locke learned Latin, Greek and Hebrew. Westminster had long-standing links with Christ Church (Oxford), and he entered the college in 1652. At the time, teaching at Oxford was still essentially scholastic, which irritated Locke, as it had Hobbes fifty years earlier. During his studies, he was content to do what was necessary to obtain his diplomas in 1656 and 1658, and devoted much of his time to reading plays, novels and epistolary correspondence, often translated from French. His interest in medicine led him to natural philosophy and to the man considered the father of modern natural philosophy, Robert Boyle, whom he met in 1660. He also met William Petty at the same university. It was also at this time that he began to read Descartes and, superficially, Gassendi.

On the death of Olivier Cromwell and during the unstable period that followed, he initially welcomed the monarchical restoration of Charles II (King of England). During this period, he published two essays in which, against one of his *Christ Church* colleagues Edward Bagshawe, he defended the idea that civil power could decide on the people's form of religion. According to Simone Goyard-Fabre, these writings express a line of thought close to that of Thomas Hobbes. In 1660, he began teaching Greek, and in 1662 rhetoric, before becoming a moral philosophy censor in 1664. In 1665, as secretary, he accompanied Sir Walter Vane on a diplomatic mission to the Elector of Brandenburg. On his return, in the summer of 1666, he met Shaftesbury, who had come to Oxford to treat his poor health with the waters of a local spring.

Serving Shaftesbury

Locke's meeting with the Earl of Shaftesbury, then Chancellor of the Exchequer to Charles II, marked a turning point in his life. The two men hit it off so well that in the spring of 1667, Locke left Oxford and followed his new mentor to London, where he became a member of his household. He continued to study medicine and met Thomas Sydenham, with whom he worked closely. It was during this period that he wrote, or Sydenham wrote (authorship is unclear), *De Arte Medica*, a document that was discovered in the XIXe century. This document expresses deep skepticism about medical hypotheses (deductive science) and advocates a purely empirical (inductive) approach to medicine. In 1668, Locke saved Shaftesbury by proposing a fully successful operation to drain a liver abscess.

In 1668, he was elected a Fellow of the Royal Society, an organization in which he seems to have had little involvement. That same year he wrote a short *Essay on Toleration*, in which he took positions opposed to those of his writings of 1660-1662. In the same year, he also began a treatise on economics never before published: *Some of the Consequences that are like to follow upon Lessing of Interest to 4 Per Cent*. From 1669 to 1675, he held administrative positions with the owners of the new colony of Caroline. Although he did not write the basic text of this territory's constitution, he was certainly involved in its correction and improvement. Around 1670, he began drafting the *Essai concernant l'entendement humain (Essay on Human Understanding)*, and around 1671 wrote what are known as *drafts* A and B. In November 1672, with Shaftesbury becoming Lord Chancellor, Locke was appointed *secretary for presentations,* responsible for religious matters. A month before Shaftesbury was dismissed in November 1673, he became Secretary to the *Board of Trade and Plantations*, a position he held until 1675. In this capacity, he took an interest in the colonization of America, especially as he was a shareholder in the Royal African Company, which engaged in the slave trade.

In November 1675, he left England for a three-and-a-half-year stay in France. From January 1676 to February 1677, he lived in Montpellier, where he met two eminent Protestant physicians, Charles Barbeyrac and Pierre Magnol, as well as the Cartesian Sylvain Leroy. During his stay in Celleneuve, a village near Montpellier, from June to September 1676, he resumed his philosophical research. In February 1677, he left Montpellier, visiting Toulouse and Bordeaux before arriving in Paris in June 1677. Here, he continued to work on philosophy, reading French versions of Descartes' works. He also made friends with two of Gassendi's disciples: philosopher François Bernier and Gilles de Launay. He also worked on his *Essai sur l'entendement humain* and wrote an *Essay de Intellectu*. In May 1679, he returned to England, after a further stay in Montpellier and another visit to Paris.

In 1679, Locke finds England in the midst of a serious political crisis over the succession to the throne. Shaftesbury and his supporters did not want James II (King of England) to succeed to the throne. This was the backdrop to the Papist plot. Fear of a new absolutist monarch above all led Shaftesbury in 1679 to pass the *Habeas Corpus* (making it impossible to be imprisoned without trial) and to try to pass the Exclusion Bill. The latter attempt failed, however, as Charles II (King of England) dissolved Parliament, leading to a split in the Whig party between the moderates and the radicals gathered around Shaftesbury. Charles II then prosecuted Shaftesbury for treason. Shaftesbury was initially acquitted by a Grand Jury (right). However, the king appointed two Tory sheriffs. In June 1682, feeling threatened, Shaftesbury fled to Holland, where he died in January 1683. In 1683, a group of Whigs attempted to assassinate Charles II and his potential successor James, the Rye-House Plot. It is not known to what extent Locke was involved in these events, but it is generally assumed that he knew enough to be worried. He therefore preferred to travel to the west of England, arranging to smuggle money to Holland before reaching that country himself. It is now generally accepted that it was during the crisis of 1679-1683 that Locke began his First Treatise, after buying a copy of Robert Filmer's *Patriarcha*. It was then that he wrote the bulk of the *Two Treatises of Civil Government*.

The last few years

In Holland, Locke made contact with other political exiles, such as Thomas Dare, one of the financiers of the

Monmouth Rebellion. In 1684, he was dismissed from *Christ Church*; in May 1685, even before the rebellion, he was placed on a list of exiles to be arrested by the Dutch government. Locke went into hiding until May 1685. During the winter of 1685-1686, he wrote *Espitola de Tolerantia*, which was published in Gouda in 1689. The triggering event seems to have been the revocation of the Edict of Nantes in 1685. The Glorious Revolution enabled him to return to England in 1689. There, he met Newton, who had been elected a member of parliament by Cambridge University. He corresponded with him on many subjects. In December 1689, he published his *Two Treatises on Government* (dated 1690 on the title page), and in May 1689 contacted a publisher for his *Essay on Human Understanding*. He also published an English translation of his *Epistola de Tolerantia*, originally written in Latin to ensure its European distribution. In April 1690, this provoked a vigorous reply from an Oxford clergyman, prompting him to reply with a *Second Letter* (1691) and then a *Third Letter* (1692).

From 1691, he lived with Sir Francis Masham, whose wife, Ralph Cudworth's daughter, had been a friend and correspondent of Locke's for many years. In July 1693, he published *Some Thoughts concerning Education*, followed the same year by *Some Considerations of the Consequences of the Lowering of Interest and Raising the Value of Monney*. John Norris (philosopher), an admirer of

Malebranche, having published critical remarks on the *Essai sur l'entendement humain*, he replied in 1692 with a rather harsh text, *JL Answer to Norris's Reflection*, followed by two more substantial writings, *Remarks upon Some of Mr Norris's Book* and *An Examination of P;Malebranche's Opinion of Seeing All Things in God*. In 1696, he was appointed a member of the *Coucil For Trade and Plantations*, a position he held until 1700. In 1696, Edward Stillingfleet, Bishop of Worcester, published *Discourse in Vindication of the Doctrine of the Trinity* with a preface in which he attacked John Toland and criticized Locke. The latter replied in 1697 with *A letter to the Right Reverend, Lord Bishop of Worcester*, which led to a reply from the bishop in May entitled *An Answer to Mr Locke's Letter*. In response, Locke wrote *Mr Locke's Reply to the Right Reverend the Lord Bishop of Worcester's Answer to his letter*, which in turn replied two months later with *An Answer to Mr Locke's Second letter*. Locke's *Reply to the Right Révérend the Lord Bishop of Worcester's Answer to his second letter,* published at the end of 1698, brought the controversy to an end, as Stillingfleet died in March 1699.

Locke spent the last four years of his life peacefully, devoting himself, when his health permitted, to his last work *Paraphrase and Notes on the Epistles of St Paul*. In 1702, he also wrote *The Discourse of Miracles*, and in the last months of his life began a *Fourth Letter on Toleration*.

He died on October 28, 1704, and was buried three days later in the parish cemetery at High Laver.

The foundations of Locke's thought

These foundations are to be found in the *Essay on Human Understanding,* one of the first great books of empiricism. In this work, Locke sets out to "examine the different faculties of knowledge which are met with in man", so as to be able to mark "the limits of the certainty of our knowledge, and the foundations of the opinions which are seen to reign among men".

Overview of the *Essay on Human Understanding*

The *Essay on Human Understanding consists of* four books preceded by a foreword. Book I, *On Innate Notions*, is centered on a rejection of innateism and nativism. Locke argues, mainly against Descartes, the Cartesians and the rationalists, that there are no innate principles. Book II, *On Ideas*, develops the thesis that ideas, the material of knowledge, come from experience alone. Book III, *On Words*, deals with language; its nature, its links with ideas and its role in the process of knowledge. Finally, Book IV, *On Knowledge*, is devoted to the nature and limits of knowledge.

The theory of ideas

In the foreword to the *Essay on Human Understanding*, Locke states that he uses the word idea to designate "whatever is the object of our understanding when we think", adding "I have therefore used it to express what may be understood by 'phantasm', 'notion', 'species', or whatever the mind may employ itself in thinking". He adds that "every man being convinced in himself that he thinks, and what is in his mind when he thinks, [are] ideas that occupy him at present".

The word "idea" is to be taken in its Cartesian and modern sense, as the totality of cognitive states or activities. It follows that Locke's idea can be perceived according to two theories: either as a psychological act, or as the object of a psychological act. This distinction places Locke among the exponents of either direct or indirect realism. The thesis of ideas as mental acts is not very controversial (thinking "with ideas"), whereas that of ideas as internal objects is much more so (thinking "at ideas"). The ambiguity is present in this passage from Book II.viii.7-8.

"But in order to better discover the nature of nosideas, and to discuss them in a more intelligible way, it is necessary to distinguish between them insofar as they are perceptions and ideas in our mind, and insofar as they are in bodies modifications of matter that produce these perceptions in the mind. (...) That if I sometimes speak of these ideas as if they were in the things themselves, it must be supposed that I mean by them the qualities which are met with in the objects which produce these ideas in us. (...) I call *idea* everything which the mind perceives in itself: and I call *quality* of the subject, the power or faculty [*power*] which there is to produce a certain idea in the mind."

This distinction is one of the major debates of the 17th century, between Malebranche and Arnaud in particular, following Descartes, for whom the notion of idea has a double meaning: "idea" as the act of thinking, and "idea" as the object of such an act.

The critique of innate ideas

Locke devotes Book I to rejecting inneism, in particular the theory that our souls passively contain ideas independently of experience. For Hamou, this criticism is aimed at "Descartes and the Cartesians", while Locke also takes aim at non-Cartesian inneists, notably Herbert de Cherbury, whose work *De veritate* he cites, and the Cambridge Platonists. He would also target "a whole group of petty authors, pamphleteers in favor of a dogmatic conception of religion and a politics based on the innate recognition of hierarchy and authority".

Locke's arguments against innate ideas are both empirical and theoretical. Seven arguments can be distinguished in

Book I against innate ideas: lack of universal consent, lack of constituents in children, ignorance of said innate ideas, need to teach some of said innate ideas, need for a minimum age to understand them, plethora of allegedly innate ideas and lack of a list.

Leibniz criticizes this thesis in his "*New Essays on Human Understanding*". Locke is part of the modern empiricist movement. In this, he foreshadows Berkeley and Hume. If God did not give men innate ideas, he did give them faculties of perception and reflection that enable them to live with dignity.

Locke now needs to explain where all ideas come from, if none of them are innate: this is the aim of Book II. His thesis is that all our ideas come from experience. Initially, the human being is a *tabula rasa,* as explained at the beginning of Book II.i.2.

"Suppose, then, that in the beginning the soul is what we call a white paper, empty of all characters and without any ideas whatsoever. How does it come to receive ideas? By what means does it acquire the prodigious quantity of ideas that man's imagination, ever active and boundless, presents to it in almost infinite variety? Where does it draw all this material, which is the basis of all its reasoning and knowledge? To this I answer in a word, from experience: it is the foundation of all our knowledge, and it is from there that it derives its first origin".

According to Locke, there are two types of experience: sensation, what our senses receive from the external world; and reflection, an introspection into the ideas of sensation. The activity of the senses is therefore primary, making Locke a true empiricist. What's more, he justifies his theory of the origin of ideas with empirical examples, such as the Molyneux problem.

Simple and complex ideas

For Locke, the simple idea "is free from all composition, and consequently produces in the soul only one entirely uniform conception [one uniform Appearance] which cannot be distinguished into different ideas". They "are the materials of all our knowledge, [and] are suggested to the soul only by the two ways of which we have spoken above, I mean by sensation, and by reflection". Locke gives examples of simple ideas: those of the sensible qualities of objects, and those of reflection. The simple ideas of the sensible qualities of objects (colors, sensation of hot, cold, hard, bitter, sweet) are transmitted to the mind by the senses. There are also simple ideas that come neither purely from the senses, nor purely from reflection, but from a mixture of the two, such as the ideas of pleasure, unity, power, existence. It's important to note that, for Locke, every simple idea present to our mind has its source in experience.

Complex ideas are made up of several simple ideas. They can be imposed on our minds by the senses. For example, the idea we have of an apple is complex, because it is made up of the ideas of color, size, etc. Other complex ideas can be created by the mind, which is then active and can produce ideas that are not present in the mind. Other complex ideas can be created by the mind, which is then active and can produce ideas that do not have a pre-existing reality: for example, the idea of fabulous monsters. For Locke, the mind can create complex ideas through two processes: the process of composition, which leads to complex ideas of substances or modes, and the process of relating simple ideas.

Abstract and general ideas

Alongside the mind's actions of composing and relating, it also abstracts, leading to generalization. Locke argues that if words are the outward sign of ideas, and if these ideas correspond only to particular things, then the number of words would be infinite. But, "to prevent this inconvenience, the mind makes general the particular ideas it has received through particular objects, which it does by considering these ideas as appearances separated from all other things....this is what is called abstraction, by which ideas drawn from some particular being becoming general, represent all beings of that species, so that the general names we give them, may be applied to everything in beings actually existing suitable to these abstracted ideas".

In his book, Locke doesn't go into much detail about the abstraction process itself, but is more prolific about the abstract ideas produced. According to Chappell, this is because, for Locke, generalizations are purely a mental process. In nature, there is only the particular. For Locke, general ideas play the same role as universals and forms or essences did for his predecessors. Locke distinguishes two ways of proceeding with abstraction, leading to two kinds of abstract ideas. In the first case, set out in Book II, the abstract idea is the simple idea of a sensible quality, whereas in the second case, set out in Book III, an abstract idea is a complex idea obtained by eliminating a number of simple ideas. For example, when we speak of a man, this is a complex idea obtained by removing all the simple ideas that enable us to distinguish one man from another.

Idea, reality and truth

For Locke (E, XXX, 1), real ideas "have a foundation in nature; [and] ... conform to a being really, to the existence of things, or to their archetypes". In contrast, fantastic or chimerical ideas are "those which have no foundation in nature, nor any conformity with the reality of the things to which they tacitly relate as to their archetypes".

Locke also distinguishes between adequate or complete ideas, which "perfectly represent the originals [archetypes] from which the mind supposes them to be derived", and incomplete ideas, which "represent only a part of the originals [archetypes] to which they relate". For Locke, truth is the opposite of falsity; truth is not, strictly speaking, a property of ideas, but only a judgment. However, when an idea is judged or assumed to conform to something external to it, it alone can be called true.

The philosophy of bodies

The corpuscular conception of bodies

In his *Essay on Human Understanding*, Locke develops a corpuscular conception of bodies rooted in the atomism of Democritus, Epicurus and Lucretius, revised in the 17th^e century by Pierre Gassendi. In England, these ideas were taken up by Robert Boyle, Thomas Hobbes and Walter Charleton' . The main principles of this conception of bodies are as follows:

1. "The matter of all bodies is of the same kind, namely, an extended solid substance;

2. "all bodies are either (a) atoms or physically indivisible individual atoms whose only qualities (apart from that of extent and solidity) are size, shape, location, motion or rest, and number, or (b) aggregates or collections of atoms" ;

3. "all changes in body states are due to changes in texture,... and any change in texture is the result of an impact or contact of one body on another".

Theories of competing bodies in the XVIIe century

According to Eduard Jan Dijksterhuis, in the mid 17th^{e} century, there were four opposing theories on the structure of matter.

Locke neglects alchemy and concentrates his attacks on Cartesian and Scholastico-Aristotelian doctrine. Locke's philosophy of bodies is called mechanical philosophy because it assumes that all phenomena can be explained either by the impact of one body on another or by motion. Proponents of mechanistic philosophy reject the notion of occult qualities or remote causes from the Aristotelian and Scholastic traditions.

Primary and secondary qualities

The distinction between primary and secondary qualities dates back to the Greek atomists. Before Locke, it was taken up by Galileo, Descartes and Robert Boyle. The primary qualities of an object or body are those it possesses independently of everything else: space occupied, being in motion or at rest, being solid, texture. Secondary qualities are the powers that bodies possess to provoke the creation of ideas in us: color, smell, etc. This distinction between primary and secondary qualities runs counter to the Scholastico-Aristotelian tradition, in which the qualities of objects are real.

Locke, like Descartes, accepts a dualism of quality, but unlike the French philosopher, this dualism does not imply a dualism of substance, since a thing can have both primary and secondary qualities. There is no substance linked to primary qualities and substance linked to secondary qualities.

The philosophy of mind

While Locke accepts Cartesian dualism, between body and mind, he differs from it by not defining the mental realm, and by not being concerned with causal interactions between the material and mental realms.

Perception and will

For Locke, the two great actions of our mind (he uses the word soul instead) are "perception, or the power of thinking, and will [volition], or the power of willing". Understanding is understood as "the power of thinking".

The action of thinking is based on ideas. The mind must verify our beliefs and *preconceptions in order* to arrive at true knowledge.

"The way in which the mind receives these kinds of propositions, is what we call *belief, assent* or *opinion*; which consists in receiving a proposition for true on evidence that presently persuades us to receive it as true, without our having a certain knowledge that it actually is. And the difference between *probability* and *certainty, between faith and knowledge,* consists in the fact that in all parts of knowledge there is intuition, so that each immediate idea, each part of the deduction has a visible and certain connection, instead of, with regard to what is called *belief*, that which makes me *believe*, is something foreign to what I believe, something which is not obviously joined to it at both ends, and which thereby does not obviously show the suitability or unsuitability of the ideas in question (Locke E, IV, 15, 3)".

For Locke, what determines the will and leads us to action is the anxiety caused by desire, desire being in fact "a state of anxiety". Initially, Locke believed that our actions were determined by the fact that we were seeking "the greatest positive good". He would later consider this to be a mistake:

"However, after a more exact investigation, I feel forced to conclude, that the good and the greatest good though judged and recognized as such, do not determine the will, unless coming to desire it in a manner proportionate to its excellence, this desire does not make us anxious that we are deprived of it (Locke, E, II, 21, 35)."

The link between mind and matter

In Book II of the *Essay*, Locke defends the notion of an immaterial thinking substance, in opposition to Hobbes' radical materialism. For Locke, there is a double link between mind and matter: the mind (soul) can act on the body, and vice versa.

" ....The need to decide for or against the immateriality of the soul is not as great as some people, too passionate about their own feelings, have tried to persuade us; some of whom, with their minds too deeply embedded, so to speak, in matter, cannot grant any existence to that which is not material; and others, not finding that thought is enclosed within the natural faculties of matter, after examining it in every sense with all the application they are capable of, are confident of concluding from this that God himself could not give life and perception to a solid substance. But whoever considers how difficult it is to combine sensation with an extended matter, and existence with a thing that has absolutely no extension, will confess that he is very far from certainly knowing what his soul is."

Spirit, personal identity and substance

For Locke, a person is "a thinking and intelligent being, capable of reason and reflection, and who can consult himself as the same, as the same thing that thinks in different times and places". According to him, it is "consciousness that makes the unity of the person". Locke, unlike Hume, insists on the unity of the person across time. Whereas for Descartes, thought constitutes the essence of mind, just as extension constitutes the entire essence of matter, for Locke things are somewhat different. According to him, what differentiates man is the fact that he is capable of thinking, not the fact that he is constantly thinking. A thing is not only a portion of matter, but also, like a watch, "an organization or construction of parts suitable to a certain end, which it is capable of fulfilling, when it receives the impression of sufficient force for it". For Locke, what characterizes man is his ability to think, and the fact that he is a body with a particular extent and organization.

Locke's philosophy of language

The importance of communication for Locke

Locke insists on the importance of communication in human progress. In the *Essays* (III,ii,1) he writes:

"Since the advantages and conveniences of society cannot be enjoyed without a communication of thoughts, it was necessary for man to invent some outward and sensible signs by which these invisible ideas of which his thoughts are composed, might be manifested to others."

Unlike Aristotle, Locke believes that there is no natural connection between certain sounds and certain ideas. The fact that words have no natural connection with the things they refer to, but are arbitrarily chosen to represent ideas about things, makes communication problematic. So we must always make sure we are understood. We mustn't assume that our words have some secret connection with the reality of things. Words come from the work of human beings, not the gods. So Locke argues that human beings must take "care to appropriate their words, as far as possible, to the ideas which ordinary use has assigned to them".

Locke versus Plato and Aristotle

Locke's breaking of the natural link between word and idea is part of an attack on Platonism, which was enjoying a revival in England at the time. Above all, it is an attack on two important points of Aristotelian science. Firstly, he opposes the Stagirite's underlying assumption that the qualities of objects most important to our perception are also the most fundamental to science. Secondly, he attacks Aristotle's assumption that classifications of natural objects into species reflect an underlying natural reality. For Locke, "species are the work of the understanding,.... they are founded on the resemblance of things".

The philosophy of knowledge

Locke was attracted by certain aspects of the new science, notably Cartesian rationalism, and saw little use in the scholastic discussions still in vogue at Oxford University.

Locke's notion of knowledge

For Locke, knowledge derives from experience. This means that all the ideas and materials from which our knowledge is fashioned by our reason derive from experience. If God has not "engraved certain ideas in the souls of all men", he has given them "faculties sufficient to make them discover all the things necessary to a being such as man, in relation to his true destination".

Knowledge "is nothing other than the perception of the connection and convenience, or of the opposition and disconvenience, between two ideas". This definition is very different from that of Descartes, for whom knowledge is a clear idea. Locke distinguishes four kinds of relations in human knowledge:

- identity or diversity (logic): two things are the same or different ;

- relation (mathematical) also called relative: it is the "perception of the relation that exists between two ideas, of whatever kind they may be, substances, modes or others";

- coexistence , or necessary (physical) connection ;

- real existence (metaphysics).

The three degrees of knowledge

For Locke, there are three degrees of knowledge: intuitive, demonstrative and sensitive.

Intuitive knowledge is the immediate perception of the suitability or unsuitability of ideas, without any intermediate idea. For example, the mind "sees that white is not black".

Demonstrative knowledge consists in comparing ideas and perceiving their suitability or unsuitability by means of other ideas that are proofs for the demonstration. Demonstrative knowledge depends on evidence, and is not easy to acquire. It is preceded by some doubt and is not as clear as intuitive knowledge. Moreover, each degree of deduction must be known intuitively. In the domain of demonstration, mathematics is the highest degree of certainty, since it comprises all four degrees.

We intuitively conceive the abstract ideas of mathematics, and these clear, distinct intuitions enable us to deduce properties. The realm of experience, on the other hand, provides no such ideas; there is nothing certain and universal there, everything is contingent. In the realm of demonstration, Locke also places the proof of God's existence; it is, according to him, the only existence that can be proved, and with a certainty equal to that of mathematics. Indeed, if we consider our existence, we know that some real being exists; and if non-being can produce nothing, then there is a being that exists from all eternity.

Sensory knowledge establishes the existence of particular beings that exist outside us, based on the ideas we have of them. This knowledge goes beyond probability, but falls short of the degrees of certainty of intuitive and demonstrative knowledge.

Knowledge, probability and judgment

For Locke, "man would be in a sad state, if he could derive [for the guidance of his life] only from those things which are founded on the certainty of true knowledge", which is why God "has provided us also, with respect to the greater part of the things which concern our own interests, an obscure light and a mere twilight of probability, if I may so express myself, in keeping with the state of mediocrity and trial in which it has pleased him to place us in this world, in order thereby to repress our presumption and the excessive confidence we have in ourselves". When knowledge is not certain, he invites us to resort to judgment, which "consists in presuming that things are in a certain way, without perceiving them with certainty".It should be noted that Locke uses the term probability not in the mathematical sense then emerging, but in the ancient sense of conformity to our observations and experience.

Reason and faith

For Locke, "as soon as reason fails any man of any sect, he at once cries out, here is an article of faith, and that is above reason." If revelation can be useful where reason cannot lead to certainty, it must not contradict what we know by reason to be true.

Locke also deals with enthusiasm, which was one of the main characteristics of certain Protestant sects at the time. In Book IV, Chapter XIX of the *Essay on Human Understanding,* he insists that to arrive at true knowledge, one must love the truth. The infallible proof of this love being "not to receive a proposition with more assurance, than the proofs on which it is founded allow." Yet, in his view, enthusiasm leads to a violation of this principle.

The limits of Locke's knowledge and mechanical philosophy

For McCann, Locke is alone among the proponents of mechanistic philosophy in the seventeenth[e] century in emphasizing the limits of our ability to provide mechanistic explanations of natural phenomena. This question is mainly dealt with in Book IV, Chapter III of the *Essay on Human Understanding*:

"Therefore we do not put this knowledge at too low a price, if we do not modestly think within ourselves that we are so far from forming an idea of the whole nature of the Universe, and understanding all the things it contains, that we are not even capable of acquiring a philosophical knowledge of the bodies which are around us, and which are part of ourselves, since we cannot have a universal certainty of their second qualities, their powers, and their operations. Our senses perceive different effects every day, of which we have hitherto a sensitive knowledge: but for the causes, manner and certainty of their production, we must resolve to ignore them for the two reasons we have just proposed."

Sifte Viator.

Hic juxta fitus eft,

JOHANNES LOCKE

Si qualis fuerit rogas, mediocritate fuâ contentum fe vixiffe refpondet. Literis innutritus eoufq; tantum profecit, ut veritate unice litaret: hoc ex fcriptis illius difce; quæ quod de eo reliquum eft, majori fide tibi exhibebunt, quam epitaphii fufpecta elogia. Virtutes fi quas habuit, minores fane quam quas fibi laudi tibi in exemplum proponeret; Vitia una fepeliantur. Morum exemplum fi quæras, in Evangelio habes, vitiorum utinam nufquam, mortalitatis certe (quod profit) hic et ubiq;.

Natum Anno Dom. 1632. Aug. 29°.
Mortuum Anno Dom. 1704. Oct. 28°.
memorat hæc tabula brevi et
ipfa interitura.

Political philosophy

Locke's political philosophy is considered a founding stage of liberal thought. This modernity is sometimes contested; the reasons for this will be explained below.

Initially, this political philosophy can be described in four parts: natural law; property; slavery; liberalism.

Natural law

Locke describes the state of nature as "a state in which men find themselves as men, and not as members of a society." (*Treatise on Civil Government*, §14) Indeed, no man is by nature subject to anyone else, for one cannot be subject to the arbitrary will of another man, nor be required to obey laws that another would institute for him.

In this state, men are free and equal. In the state of nature, no one has legislative authority. Equality is a consequence of this freedom, for if there is no natural relationship of personal subjection, it is due to the absence of distinction between men: all have the same faculties.

Nevertheless, the freedom of this state is not licentious; everyone is obliged to make the best use of it for his own preservation (§4). The state of nature therefore already contains certain rules. Although there is no humanly instituted law, all men must nevertheless obey the law of nature, a law discovered by reason (or revelation) and of divine origin. This law forbids men to do whatever they wish; they have a duty :

- to preserve their own life, which is a gift from God (§6);

- to respect the life, liberty and property of others, because it is necessary for their preservation that each person look after the subsistence of humankind once his own is assured;

- to strive to lead a peaceful and harmonious life with others; violence is thus forbidden, except to defend oneself or others (§7);

- to keep promises and perform contracts (§14).

Freedom lies in respect for these obligations prescribed by the laws of nature, for it is by obeying them that man is led to do what is in accordance with his nature and his interests. Freedom is therefore not the absence of external obstacles to the realization of one's desires, but obedience to the divine prescriptions discovered by reason.

The property

The transition from natural law to property (in the broadest sense) is made by law. Indeed, insofar as man has natural duties, he is also the bearer of rights designed to guarantee him the possibility of fulfilling his duties. His rights are therefore natural, linked to his person, because they are founded on his human nature, on what is required to fulfill what he is naturally destined to do, as revealed to him by divine law.

Locke sets out three fundamental rights: the right to life and to found a family; the right to liberty; the right to enjoy one's possessions and, above all, to exchange them.

These rights define a domain of inviolability for the human person; their natural character excludes the legitimacy of exchanging them, or of not recognizing them by convention.

Among these rights, which precede all human institutions, Locke places the enjoyment of property. Private property is necessary for the preservation of life and the exercise of human dignity. There is therefore a right to possess everything necessary for subsistence.

Nevertheless, since the world was given to mankind in common by God, we need to explain the legitimacy of individual appropriation:

"Although the earth and all lower creatures belong in common to all men, each man is nevertheless the owner of his own person. No one but himself has a right to it; the labor of his body and the work of his hands belong to him alone. He mingles his labor with everything he brings out of the state in which nature has left it, and adds something of his own to it. In so doing, he makes it his property. This thing being extracted by him from the common being in which nature had placed it, his work adds something to it, which excludes the common right of other men." (§27)

It is this labor-based ownership that allows Locke to justify the colonists' seizure of Native American lands. Since the Indians don't work their land and don't respect God's commandment (*Second Treatise on Civil Government*, V, 32), whoever exploits them automatically acquires ownership. And if an Indian violently opposes this spoliation through work, he is "quite comparable, like any criminal, to the 'wild beasts near which the human being knows neither society nor security'; 'he can therefore be destroyed like a lion, like a tiger'".

Man is therefore the sole owner of his person and body, and enjoys exclusive property rights. He is also the owner of his work: a thing worked ceases to be common property:

"Thus, the grass my horse eats, the clods of earth my valet has pulled up, and the hollows I have made in places to which I have a common right with others, become my own property and inheritance, without anyone's consent." (§28)

There is, however, a limit to the legitimacy of this private appropriation, and that is that it must :

"remain enough, of as good a quality, and even more than could be used by individuals who were not yet provided for." (§33)

But once we've explained the idea of property through work, we still need to explain how man is the owner of his person? Locke defines the person as follows:

"It is, I think, a thinking and intelligent being endowed with reason and reflection, and which can consider itself as the same thinking thing in different times and places. This only comes from that *consciousness* which is inseparable from thinking, and which is essential to it, as it seems to me: for it is impossible for anyone to perceive without also perceiving that he perceives." (*Essay on Human Understanding*, II, 27, 9).

Personal identity is founded on the continuity of consciousness over time, and this consciousness constitutes the identity that, by means of memory, is maintained over time and enables us to recognize ourselves as being the same.

But this capacity of consciousness :

- is fundamentally appropriative, since it allows us to recognize actions and thoughts as our own, *i.e.* to identify an agent responsible to men and to the creator.

- founds the property of the self, in particular of the body which is the body of so-and-so, and which thus presents itself to his consciousness (through his actions and their results).

To sum up Locke's thinking on property, we can say that the ownership of things is not only required for subsistence, but is an extension of the ownership of the person. In this sense, property ownership has the same inviolable character as the human person. This person is conceived as a relationship of self to self as property. Every human being is therefore the sole owner of his person, his life, his freedom and his property.

Liberalism

Locke's thought can be seen as the founding thought of liberalism, both politically and economically.

Locke's politics of liberalism

On the political level, Locke's question is whether political power can be thought of without its institution leading to the loss of liberty of the individuals subject to it.

As Locke sees men in the state of nature as property owners, they are engaged in economic relations; this point already tends to lead to the conception of a state that would be content to guarantee what is acquired, without intervening in society. Political power is therefore not supposed to institute social order through laws, but to serve society by correcting elements that tend to harm it.

It follows that political power :

- originates in the consent of those over whom authority is exercised;

- has its end in guaranteeing respect for the natural rights of every man, that it must arbitrate conflicts and exercise a right to punish.

In Traité du gouvernement civil, chapter VII, *De la société politique ou civile*; he writes as follows:

"Men therefore leave the state of nature, and enter into a political society, when they create and establish judges (legislative power) and Sovereigns on earth, to whom they communicate the authority to end all disputes (executive power), and to punish all insults that may be done to any of the members of society; and wherever we see a certain number of men, in whatever way they may have associated themselves, among whom there is no such decisive power, to which we may appeal, we must regard the state in which they are, as always being the state of nature".

In political society, "each member has divested himself of his natural power, and placed it in the hands of society".

Political power is thus stripped of its ethical and religious dimensions; it cannot prohibit worship, it is not concerned with the salvation of men or their moral perfection. These are strictly personal matters. The state is therefore an instrument, and its role is reduced to the civil and temporal interests of men, whose life, liberty and property it must protect.

With its scope thus limited, Locke proposes a hierarchy of powers, an institutional organization to control their exercise, and consequently asserts that the people have the right (indeed, the obligation) to resist when power exceeds the limits assigned to it by its function.

The hierarchy of power

The social contract creates a community that is the sole holder of all powers. But since it cannot exercise these powers itself, they are delegated to magistrates. In any political organization, there is a part that defines what each power must do, and a part that designates the holders of these powers, who are obeyed.

While the use of force concerns the executive and federal powers, the legislative power belongs to society itself. For Locke, legislative power is the supreme power: it cannot therefore be absolute and arbitrary:

- positive law is subordinate to the laws of nature;

- this power is the pooling of the power of individuals: there can be no superior power;

- this power is universal, not directed at individuals as such;

- it is a stable and public power, it establishes a regular legal order;

- it is impossible for the legislative power to deprive a man of his property, because this property is inviolable ;

- the legislative power has only the power to make laws, and is absolutely dependent on the community: only the latter has the right to appoint legislative bodies and the right to control their exercise.

In Locke's view, the hierarchy of powers consists in subordinating executive power to legislative power, since the latter is the supreme power and the expression of the will of a community. Rule and law therefore have primacy, and no one is above the law. The executive power is therefore naturally inferior, as it only executes the decisions of the legislative power. The federal power, as a third power, remains inferior and independent of the legislative and executive powers. It concerns foreign affairs and relations with other countries: military, monetary, economic and commercial. Locke considers this power natural, because it is exercised within the framework of the positive laws of the Commonwealth, which are exclusively internal.

To avoid the concentration of power, it should be delegated to separate bodies, or even to several bodies with the same power; for example, the legislature can belong to an assembly and to the king. But it is preferable to entrust all or part of this power to an elected and renewable assembly, so that no individual in society is privileged.

However, this type of organization carries with it the risk of abuse, both of executive and legislative power. According to Locke, whatever happens, and even if power has been delegated, the community is still the only true holder of these powers. Consequently, it has the right to control the exercise of these powers, and is the sole judge in the matter. If legislative power is abused, the community declares the decisions of the judicial body to be null and void, and the latter is thereby dissolved.

Right of resistance

Since there can be abuse, even oppression, and since the community can never be deprived of its rights, it must also have the right to resist oppression.

Locke distinguishes three cases where the right of resistance applies:

- betrayal of a magistrate (e.g. use of force outside the law: usurpation, tyranny);

- when a magistrate neglects his duties;

- on evidence of a treasonous plot.

The community then has the right to judge, and when someone wants to exercise a power for which they have not been designated (i.e. when someone wants to exercise a power that does not exist), disobedience is legitimate.

The question of slavery

According to David B. Davis, in keeping with his conceptions of property and the natural law revealed by the Christian God, Locke "is the last great philosopher who sought to justify absolute and perpetual slavery". Thus:

"every free citizen of Carolina exercises unlimited power and authority over his black slaves, regardless of their opinions or religion." (*Fundamental Constitutions of Carolina*)

On a theoretical level, according to Domenico Losurdo, it was with Locke that slavery was established on a racial basis. The conversion of slaves remains subordinate to the right of ownership and does not imply their emancipation:

"Christian religion and freedom have in no way altered the condition of men in the city [and] slaves, however submissive they may be to the pact of Christ, are no less civilly slaves, and owe their masters the same obedience as before." (*The Civil Magistrate*)

While Locke supports the institution of slavery in his legal and legislative texts, his works of political philosophy (notably the Second *Treatise on Civil Government*) seek to demonstrate that no man has an absolute right over another, with the consequence that life, property, liberty and health belong to us alone and constitute a limit to the action of others. By virtue of the natural law theorized by Locke, slavery is therefore illegitimate:

"The state of nature has the law of nature, which must regulate it, and to which everyone is obliged to submit and obey: reason, which is this law, teaches all men, if they are willing to consult it, that being all equal and independent, no one must harm another, in relation to his life, his health, his liberty, his good."

Jean Fabre argues that slavery is unnatural for Locke.

John Locke was a shareholder in the Royal African Company, one of the pillars of the development of the slave trade.

Women's place

Although individual freedom is at the heart of Locke's political thought, he does not extend it to women, whom he asserts to be subject to men. To support this assertion, Locke relies on biblical texts, in particular the First Epistle to the Corinthians, which he analyzes in *Paraphrase and Notes on the first Epistle of St Paul to the Corinthians* in 1706. Theologian Mary Astell reacted by referring the biblical text to Christian morality, not philosophy. In her view, the Bible should be a guide for the individual, but cannot be invoked to resolve philosophical debates.

Religion and tolerance in Locke

Locke's writings in context

Locke wrote four major works on toleration: the *Tracts of 1660*, the *Essay on Tolerance* written in 1667, a text entitled *On the Difference between Ecclesiastical and Civil Power* of 1674, and the *Letter on Tolerance* of 1686. Locke's abiding interest in this question can be explained by the challenges of the time. He lived at a time when the Wars of Religion were not completely over. France revoked the Edict of Nantes in 1685, while in England the religious aspect was very present in the two revolutions that shook the country in the XVIIe century. In fact, in England, the reform undertaken by Henry VIII Tudor with the creation of the Anglican Church led to the Church being confined to helping the eternal salvation of its faithful, and being deprived of judicial and legislative powers. In this respect, politics was ahead of the theoretical writings of Althusius, Grotius and Hobbes. However, Henry VII's reform meant that civil government could sanction religious offenses such as false beliefs. In fact, Henry VIII Tudor's Anglican reform posed problems for Catholics, because they were excluded from politics, and for Protestants, because the king could impose "the content of belief and the form of worship", and the Church remained highly hierarchical. However, many Protestant theologians, such as Thomas Cartwright and Robert Browne, maintain that the Church is a voluntary association, that conscience and conviction alone count, and that in these circumstances the State has no business interfering. John Penry, the probable author of the *Marprelate Tracts,* writes: "Neither prison, nor judgments, nor death itself can be suitable weapons for convincing the consciences of men which are founded on the word of God alone". According to Jean-Fabien Spitz, "very early on (...) the main themes of the argument in favor of tolerance were established". Among them was the idea that the State was concerned only with the temporal, not with the salvation of souls, that the Church was merely an association of conviction, that it could exclude members but not prosecute them in the temporal sphere. Writings advocating these ideas before Locke include William Walwyn's *The Compassionate Samaritan: Liberty of Conscience Asserted and the Separatist Vindicated* (1644) in John Goodwin's pamphlet *Hagiomatix* (1646).

Writings on tolerance

The *tracts* of 1660 and the *Essay on tolerance* 1667

Locke first wrote about tolerance in 1660, in response to Edward Bagshaw's *The great question concernant things indifferent in religious worship.* To understand the nature of the problem, we need to place this writing in context. Some Protestants wanted to place political organization under the aegis of God's law, and distinguished between points on which the Gospels were explicit and those on which they were silent, such as the form of worship. While they considered the latter to be a matter solely for the freedom of conscience and the liberty of the Christian, for them civil government had to intervene where the Gospels were precise. For Jean-Fabien Spitz, "in the face of such a conception, Locke manifests in the two *Tracts* of 1660 a concern that will never leave him, and whose mark the *Epistola* will still bear": the impossibility, under these conditions, of establishing a political civil authority. For Locke, as for the latitudinarians, since indifferent things have no influence on the salvation of men, they can be regulated in the best temporal interests of men, and where necessary entrusted to civil government. Locke even goes so far as to consider that the government can impose uniformity of worship if it deems it necessary for peace. In fact, he goes to this extreme because for him "religion is reduced to a few fundamental articles, to inward repentance and to a charity that governs a virtuous life". However, Locke is aware that his argument will never convince a believer who considers the exterior of worship to be of crucial importance to his salvation. Thus, for Jean-Fabien Spitz, "research into the limits of human understanding and the negative conclusions it leads to" led him to propose a policy of religious toleration in his later writings of 1667 and 1686.

The 1667 *Essay was* probably written at Shaftesbury's request. It was written in a context where the different currents of Protestantism had to live together, so that the notion of "toleration" is seen as an agreement to live together among Protestant sects, and a common commitment to fight against atheists and Catholics. Locke, like other writers on toleration at the time, was not concerned with the attitude to be adopted towards non-Christians, a problem that hardly arose in the England of his time. He presents the political advantages for the English monarchy. Coexistence between Protestants of different persuasions is seen as possible, provided there is no confrontation between theologies, and their consequences "harmful to society or to others" are rejected. This implicitly defines a natural ethic based on indifference, which is also Locke's definition of the "social contract". This essay was not published, as the political context of the Restoration made its publication risky for its author.

Letter on tolerance

For Locke, "the state is a society of men instituted for the sole purpose of establishing, preserving and advancing their civil interests". In his view, the civil magistrate, the ruler, is concerned only with the temporal. The spiritual, the religious, does not belong to his sphere of action. In support of this thesis, he puts forward three arguments. Firstly, God has given no man the mission of looking after the salvation of others. Secondly, the power of government rests solely on force, whereas true religion is in the realm of the spirit. Thirdly, even supposing that rulers can ensure salvation, rulers are diverse and so are the religions prescribed by rulers, so that not all rulers can provide salvation, since they propose different paths. It follows that the magistrate has no business dealing with religion and souls. For Jean-Fabien Spitz, "the liberal argument unfolds here explicitly: political authority has no business regulating the conduct of individuals in actions that are incapable of affecting the personal interests of others". In contrast, Jonas Proast (1640-1710), one of Locke's critics, argues that in fact only two arguments are valid. In his view, force can lead to citizens considering beliefs they would otherwise ignore. What's more, a human being always wants to promote what he believes to be true, even if he can't prove that it really is.

In any case, Locke draws a sharp distinction between civil society or the state, whose purpose "is civil peace and prosperity, or the preservation of society and of each of its members", and religious society or the church, whose object is to enable individuals "to attain happiness after this life and in the next world". While both have in common the fact that they are voluntary associations, another essential difference separates them: in the body politic, human beings are obliged to follow laws on pain of temporal sanctions (prisons, fines, etc.), whereas in the spiritual society that is the Church, only persuasion can be used, not force or violence. Under these conditions, the civil magistrate only has to punish vices if they threaten civil peace. Locke writes

"Everyone admits that avarice, harshness towards the poor, idleness and many other faults are sins, but who has ever ventured to say that the magistrate has the right to punish? As these faults do not harm the property of others, and do not disturb public peace, civil laws do not punish them in the very places where they are recognized as sins. Nor do these laws pronounce punishments against lying or perjury, unless it is in certain cases, where no consideration is given to the turpitude of the crime, nor to the divinity offended, but to the injustice done to the public or to individuals".

Locke's problem is that men invert the order of clarity, and focus on what is not essential to their salvation: questions of dogma, ceremonial forms and little virtue, and that they will ask the civil magistrate to intervene on these points and, if the magistrates give in, provoke conflict between the churches and civil society. So it's important to be firm on the distinction. Even so, there may be cases where civil prescriptions interfere with people's conscience. For Locke, this can be a case of disobedience, and while he advises following one's conscience, he stresses that one must also accept the price.

Locke's religious beliefs

Locke's political convictions are often seen by scholars as linked to his religious beliefs". If Locke in his youth was a Calvinist who believed in the trinity, by the time he published his *Reflections* (1695), he was not only adopting Socinian views on toleration, his Christology was also Socinian. However, Wainwright (1987) notes that in his posthumous *Paraphrase* (1707), the interpretation of verse 1:10 of the letter to the Ephesians marks a notable difference from that of a Socinian such as Biddle, which may indicate that by the end of his days, Locke had reverted to a belief close to Arianism accepting the preexistence of Christ. For historian John Marshall, Locke's perception of Christ at the end of his life was "somewhere between Socinism and Arianism". Although Locke was unsure about the question of original sin at the time, which also contributed to his being considered a Socinian, an Arian, or even a deist, he did not deny the reality of evil: human beings are capable of unjust war and crime. Criminals must be punished, even with the death penalty. Concerning the Bible, Locke was very conservative. He accepts the doctrine of the divine inspiration of Scripture, and miracles are proof of the divine nature of the biblical message. Locke is convinced that the entire content of the Bible is consistent with human reason (*The reasonableness of Christianity*, 1695). Although Locke is an advocate of tolerance, he urges civil authorities not to tolerate atheism, because he believes that denial of God's existence undermines social order and leads to chaos. This position rules out any attempt to deduce ethics and natural law from purely secular accuracies. For Locke, the cosmological argument is true and proves the existence of God. For Waltron, Locke's political thought is based on "*a particular set of Protestant Christian assumptions*".

Locke's conception of man is rooted in creation. We were "sent into the World by *[God's] order, and about his business, [we] are his Property, whose Workmanship [we] are, made to last during his, not one anothers Pleasure*". As with the other two major philosophers of the natural law tradition, Hugo Grotius and Samuel Pufendorf, for Locke natural law and divine revelation are two closely related concepts, since both have their source in God and therefore cannot contradict each other' . As a philosopher, Locke was deeply influenced by Christian doctrine. In his book *Reasonableness* (1695), he insists that men are unlikely to understand the precise requirements of the law of nature without the assistance of the teachings and example of Jesus. The fundamental concepts of Locke's political theory derive from biblical texts, in particular Genesis 1 and 2, the Decalogue, the (Book of Exodus 20), the Golden Rule Matthew (7:12), the teachings of Jesus and his doctrine of charity, Matthew 19:19 and the Epistles of Paul. The Decalogue in particular places a person's life, dignity and honor under God's protection. Similarly, the idea of freedom is emphasized in the Book of Exodus (liberation of the Jews from Egypt). When Locke draws the fundamental aspects of his ethics (liberty, equality, consent of the governed) from biblical texts, he does so as a philosopher, not a theologian. The U.S. Declaration of Independence follows Locke's thinking when it bases human rights partly on the biblical understanding of creation. It does the same when it bases government on the consent of the governed.

Locke's influence

Hans Aarsleff considers Locke "the most important philosopher of modern times". In his view, the phrase God "commands what reason does", found in Book IV of John Locke's works, sums up both the content and the unity of this philosopher's thought.

The father of English empiricism

His *Essay on Human Understanding* is considered to mark the beginning of what is known as English empiricism, which has long been the main mode of philosophizing for English speakers from Berkeley to Hume, from John Stuart Mill to Bertrand Russel and Alfred Jules Ayer. For Aarsleff, the philosophical thought of Locke and English empiricism :

Locke's empiricism tends to make him seen as a contradiction of René Descartes, even if his thought has certain Cartesian aspects. Locke's empiricism earned him the opposition of part of the Anglican Church - notably Stillingfleet - who saw it as a threat to the mysteries of the faith - particularly that of the Holy Trinity. In the field of natural science, Locke's empiricism led to a rejection of absolute truths. Locke points to the limits of our knowledge, human understanding and other arts, and argues that since we cannot know the real essence of substances, natural science can be neither of the same nature nor as certain as geometry.

Translation and distribution

The first translators of Locke's works into French were Jean Le Clerc, Pierre Coste and David Mazel. All three had studied theology at the Académie de Genève, were Protestants and formed a "circle of friends", according to specialist Delphine Soulard. Pierre Coste was even Locke's collaborator. The work of these three theologians led to the dissemination of Locke's philosophical and political thought in France, which had a major influence on the Enlightenment.

Voltaire's reading of the *Essai*

In his *Essay on Human Understanding,* Locke argues that we have no reason to believe that matter cannot think. This assertion is linked to what he saw as the modesty of philosophy, a point that Voltaire insisted on in his influential passage on Locke in *Lettres concernant la nation anglaise.* The problem is that the French Enlightenment philosopher's writing tends to bring Locke's philosophy closer to that of Spinoza and Hobbes, as well as deist thinkers like John Toland and Anthony Collins. As a result, for Aarlsleff, "what for Locke was an innocent remark became the subject of sharp debates between believers and non-believers, between those for whom Locke was a skeptic and those for whom he was the voice of freedom and the autonomy of the secularist". The newspapers of the time gave such prominence to these debates that Aarsleff devoted as many articles to Locke as he did to Nietzsche and Derrida at the end of the 20th[e] century. Nevertheless, all this noise tends to make Locke look like a radical skeptic, which is what earned him so much opposition in the XIX[e] century.

In addition, William Molyneux's remark led to the famous Molyneux Problem, which provoked much debate after Voltaire wrote about it in his *Elements of Newton's Philosophy*. Let's recall that the problem posed the question of whether a blind man who had been blind from birth and suddenly regained his sight could distinguish between two objects he had previously identified by touch. The question was taken up by La Mettrie, Buffon and Condillac. In England, Molyneux's problem enabled *Berkeley to* inaugurate the post-Lockian tradition of British empiricism in his *Essay toward a New Theory of Vision* (1709) and his *Treatise on the Principles of Human Kownledge.*

Influence on the encyclopedists' philosophy of language

Locke had a profound influence on the philosophy of language that developed in the 18th[e] century. For him, language is human in origin, not divine or Adamic. Words were not invented by philosophers or logicians, but by ignorant, illiterate people, who named things according to their needs and convenience. Following in his footsteps, Condillac considered that a good language could only be a perfecting of an ordinary, local language, never a perfect, universal, philosophical language. An idea taken up by Diderot in 1755 in his *Encyclopédie* article. Be that as it may, this approach to language led Locke to make etymology a branch of the history of thought, as "Words ultimately derived from such as signify sensible ideas", one of Locke's most-quoted phrases of the 18th[e] century. In 1756, Turgot took up this idea in the Encyclopédie article *Étymologie,* when he described this field of knowledge as an interesting branch of experimental metaphysics. In the same article, Turgot speaks of the torch of etymology, which helps avoid thousands of errors. This image of the torch would become extremely popular at the end of the 18th[e] century. For Aarsleff, the metaphor of the torch of etymology is a bit like entering Plato's cave with your own light.

Étienne Bonnot de Condillac admired Locke and considered him the greatest of modern philosophers. However, he believes that Locke's ideal of wordless discourse is a chimera. In his 1746 book, *Essai sur l'origine des connaissances humaines*, he stressed that language is necessary to begin to understand the world. For Condillac, languages are first and foremost poetic, as the imagination plays an important role in their development.

The world of prose, on the other hand, is one of analysis, which limits the imagination. The importance given to imagination led Diderot to emphasize genius in his *Encyclopédie* article, heralding the arrival of Romanticism. Moreover, Condillac's insistence that language can only come into being in society, according to Willard Van Orman Quine, marks a major turning point in logic, which he compares to the Copernican revolution in astronomy. After him, the natural semantic unit will no longer be the word, but the sentence.

Influence of political treaties

According to Simone Goyard-Fabre, the hallmark of Locke's political writings is their anti-absolutism, making him a "formidable anti-Bossuet". In the 18th[e] century, Locke's political writings were to be widely read, and his *Two Treatises* became, in the words of L. Stephen, quoted by Goyard-Fabre, "the political bible of the new century". In 1704, the year of his death, Pierre Coste published an *Éloge de M. Locke.* [e]In 18th-century France, Locke was seen as the founder of the theory of the social pact, and as the man who "undermined" the theory of the divine right of kings. Thanks in part to Montesquieu, Locke's liberalism was equated with constitutionalism. In fact, both Locke and Montesquieu were consecrated with the *American Declaration of Independence*. For Goyard-Fabre, while the drafters of the Bill of Rights passed in 1776 invoked Aristotle and Cicero, it was "to Sidney's *Discourses*, Locke's *Second Treatise*, Montesquieu's *Spirit of the Laws*" that they borrowed "their liberal inspiration and their constitutional breath".

In the XIXe century, Locke was cited less frequently, even though, according to Goyard-Fabre, "under Queen Victoria, Lockean liberalism was becoming not the doctrine of a party, but the philosophy of a nation, and, beyond that, the sign of an epoch in the history of the West". At the beginning of the XIXe century, Locke's liberalism came up against those who wanted to limit individualism in the name of a higher authority, such as Joseph de Maistre's Church, Hegel's State or Auguste Comte's positive science. From the People's Spring onwards, his thinking had to contend with socialism. At the end of the 20th^e century, Locke's liberalism, which according to Goyard-Fabre advocates a "moderate" state and believes "that the people, through their political participation, can themselves work out the conditions of liberty", clashes with those who have an absolute vision of liberty, who want everything to be permitted.

An eclipse in the XIXe century and a comeback in the XXe century

In the early 19th^e century, Locke's thought was widely understood as that of the Encyclopedists and Enlightenment philosophers. As such, it was held responsible for the French Revolution. Coleridge argues that the *Essays* led both to the destruction of metaphysics and to the belief among uncultured people that common sense dispensed them from study. For Thomas Carlyle, Locke led to the banishment of religion from the world. For Joseph de Maistre, Locke was the evil genius of eighteenth-century theophobia[e] , a sin for which the French Revolution was divine punishment. In the XIX[e] century, Locke was seen as a sensualist, an atheist, a materialist and a utilitarian, and in the years 1830-1840, his thought was singularly frowned upon at Cambridge University. In France, at the same time, Victor Cousin published a *Philosophie de Locke* that was widely read and considered serious. Some, such as Thomas Webb, author of *The Intellectualism of Locke* in 1857, called it "not only an insult to Locke's memory, but also to Philosophy and Common Sense". In fact, Cousin took issue with Locke's notion of ideas as the fruit of man's labor, preferring Descartes' notion of innate ideas, which he judged more compatible with religion and traditional values.

Locke only came back into favor at the end of the 19th[e] century with the American pragmatists. In 1890, Charles Sanders Peirce wrote: "Locke's great work essentially says this: men must think for themselves, and sound thinking is an act of perception. We cannot fail to recognize a superior element of truth in Locke's practical thought, which on the whole places him almost above the level of

Descartes". The same positive assessment can be found in William James. Nevertheless, a first critical edition of the *Essay on Human Understanding,* published in 1894, sold poorly. It wasn't until the 1950s that Locke's work was seriously studied. At that time, Peter Laslett's work showed that the *two treatises* had not been written after 1688, while John Dunn argued that Locke's work had been less influential in England and America than initially thought. A thesis that has had the merit of prompting researchers to better analyze Locke's influence on the XVIIIe century. John Yolton, in his 1956 book *John Locke and the Way of Ideas*, studied the reception of the work and its intellectual context. This research effort led to a new edition of Locke's works by Locke's Clarendonvaux publishing house. In 1991, the philosopher Michael Ayer published a two-volume book entitled *Locke*

Works

Works published during his lifetime

- *Essay on tolerance*, 1667

- *Anatomica*, 1668

- *De arte medica*, 1669

- Participation in the drafting of a constitution for the colony of North Carolina, never implemented, 1670

- *Letter on tolerance*, 1689

- *Essay on Human Understanding*, 1689

- *Treatise on Civil Government* (in two parts), 1690

- *Considerations on the consequences of decreasing interest and increasing the value of money* (1691)

- *Thoughts on education*, 1693

- *Reasonable Christianity*.

Posthumously published works

- *First Tract of Government* (or *the English Tract*)

- (*c.*1662) *Second Tract of Government* (or *the Latin Tract*)

- (1664) *Questions Concerning the Law of Nature* (Bilingual Latin-English edition in Robert Horwitz et al, eds, John Locke, *Questions Concerning the Law of Nature*, Ithaca: Cornell University Press, 1990).

- *An Examination of P.Malebranche's Opinion of Seeing All Things in God* (1693)

- *Of the Conduct of the Understanding* 1697

- *Discourse of Miracles* (1702)

- (1707) *A paraphrase and notes on the Epistles of St. Paul to the Galatians, 1 and 2 Corinthians, Romans, Ephesians*

- (1722) *Histoire de la navigation: son commencement, son progrès & ses découvertes* ..., tome premier, tome second.

Tributes

- (7010) Locke, asteroid named in his honor.

- John Locke, one of the main characters in the Lost: The Departed series, named in honor of the philosopher.

Other books by United Library

https://campsite.bio/unitedlibrary

ISBN 978-94-6490-062-0